The Li
INSTRUCTIO
for dogs

D1390894

Kate Freeman

summersdale

THE LITTLE INSTRUCTION BOOK FOR DOGS

Summersdale Publishers Ltd
46 West Street
Chichester
West Sussex
PO19 1RP
UK

www.summersdale.com

Printed and bound in the Czech Republic

ISBN: 978-1-84953-629-5

Substantial discounts on bulk quantities of Summersdale books are available to corporations, professional associations and other organisations. For details contact Nicky Douglas by telephone: +44 (0) 1243 756902, fax: +44 (0) 1243 786300 or email: nicky@summersdale.com.

To..

From..

The poor dog, in life the firmest friend.
The first to welcome, foremost to defend.

Lord Byron

People think a dog's life is easy: you get to lick yourself clean, somebody else picks up your poo, you're fed continuously (because you'll eat anything), and you get your very own personal trainer taking you out for exercise (without having to pay a monthly gym membership). But the truth is, being a dog is actually very hard work. And there's no instruction manual for how to be a good dog either – you just have to make it up as you go along... until now.

This book is your ultimate companion to becoming a better dog – not a good dog, or a less bad dog – but better; a dog that deserves its own place at the head of the family dinner table, not underneath it.

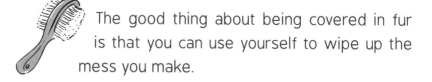 The good thing about being covered in fur is that you can use yourself to wipe up the mess you make.

You'll never be able to catch your own tail. Don't even try; it makes us look very stupid to the humans.

Don't ever apologise or feel ashamed for barking loudly when your humans are asleep. They don't realise we have superb night vision, so while they think we are barking at nothing in the dark, the reality is we see *everything* in the day AND the night.

There are three golden rules when it comes to sniffing dogs' bottoms:

 **Don't sniff a dog's bottom if you know that dog has just done a poo.**

 **Don't sniff a dog's bottom if that dog is currently sniffing another dog's bottom.**

 **Don't try to sniff your own bottom.**

Never follow a child onto a roundabout.

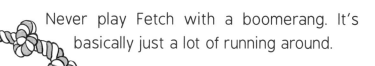 Never play Fetch with a boomerang. It's basically just a lot of running around.

Toilet water is for flushing. It is NOT for drinking.

You're going to be told to 'sit' a lot. Don't – if you're always doing what they tell you for no reward they'll think they can boss you around all the time.

Puppies have that 'new puppy smell' that makes humans fall in love with them, but don't get too jealous. Humans are fickle; they'll tire of them when they remember just how much hard work puppies are.

Eating grass and flowers turns your poo funny colours, meaning you get more fuss from your owner as they'll think you're ill. Try it!

Every time the cliché 'barking mad' is used in your presence, howl at the moon and walk out of the room in disgust.

We undoubtedly make great swimmers, but doggy paddle is hardly the most graceful of strokes. Put all your efforts into perfecting your breaststroke or the butterfly, in an attempt to become the first elegant canine swimmer.

Humans will always blame their farts on you.
Don't take it lying down. Get your own back.

The vacuum cleaner may be noisy but
it is not your enemy.

You may get to accompany your owner on exciting trips in the car. Make the journey even more fun for everyone involved by alerting them to every car, person, animal or tree that you pass. The optimum viewpoint for this activity is from the driver's lap.

Dogs like going for a walk but don't let your owner get the wrong idea and think you enjoy a run – dig your heels in and refuse to move. They'll soon give up when they realise you're not going anywhere.

If you're going to go digging up flower beds in the back garden while looking for bones, ensure that it is the most recently planted flower bed to provide maximum drama.

Watching and barking at the cars as they go by while sitting on your special spot on the window ledge is fun, but please always remember:

🦴 Cars are not 'metal dogs'.

🦴 Cars are not another form of human.

🦴 Cars are unable to communicate back to you.

Humans will use you in order to vent their frustrations. Put your head in their lap and look up at them soberly. They know you're only thinking of food, but they'll appreciate the gesture.

Humans will try to train you. Give them the impression you're an obedient dog so that they trust you, then ignore their commands completely.

 Dog poo. You may have hundreds of thousands of years of evolution telling you that you need to eat it. But you don't. You really don't.

Slippers are meant to be chewed. Don't feel bad about it.

If you're caught after having an accident indoors, use your paw to point to any small children or infants nearby, as if to suggest 'It wasn't me'.

Always join in when you see grown men kicking a ball about in the park. They may say you're ruining their game, but you know you're actually making it better.

Whenever someone in the family says 'Aren't you a good doggy?' it usually means you're about to be forced to have a bath. You've been warned!

Your owners are throwing a birthday party for their youngest daughter. The birthday cake (Victoria sponge with icing) is being brought to the dining room table, as everyone sings 'Happy Birthday'. How do you behave?

🦴 Bark 'Happy Birthday' as loudly as you can.

🦴 Sit quietly, do nothing, be well behaved.

🦴 Jump up onto the table and try to eat the entire cake in one mouthful.

Wagging your tail is a great way to communicate with humans. It's also great for knocking glasses of red wine onto the carpet. This seems to really excite the humans!

If you go camping in the woods with your family, don't – and this is a BIG NO-NO – ever let them tie a toilet roll around your neck. You're not a dispensing machine; and you should not be forced to aid them when they poo in the woods. They are meant to watch you poo, not the other way around.

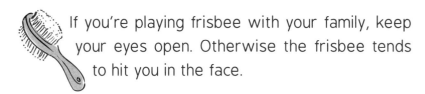

If you're playing frisbee with your family, keep your eyes open. Otherwise the frisbee tends to hit you in the face.

Washing machines are not televisions. Don't make us all look stupid by staring at your family's one for hours.

While out on your walk, if you see a dog that you fancy coming towards you, don't get all excited and start wagging your tail. Play it cool, give them some swagger:

🦴 Pretend you haven't noticed them. Let them come and sniff you out.

🦴 Give them a quick sniff, but don't linger on it.

🦴 Take more interest in a stick or fresh poo than them. Make them work hard for your affection.

Your family may give you a birthday card as a celebration of the anniversary of the day you were born. Chew it.

Whenever there is a toddler around, perch yourself nearby. There will always be crumbs and scraps dropping on the floor. Help by clearing them up before the humans can.

Your owner keeps saying it's time for 'your' walk. If it's your walk, the very minute you're off the lead GO EXPLORING! FOR HOURS! It's your walk, after all. Not theirs.

Never bite the hand that feeds you. It won't be long before you'll want it to feed you again.

Paw the TV screen every time an advert for the local steak restaurant comes on TV. Let everyone know that steak is your favourite.

Find out which family member is the most emotionally vulnerable that day and follow them around, looking sad. Your sympathetic compassion (and emotional manipulation) will earn you lots of extra doggy treats.

As one of the most loyal creatures on earth, your family will expect you to protect them when they need you the most. Sadly, this doesn't include:

🦴 Every time the doorbell rings.

🦴 When another dog comes within 100 ft.

🦴 Every time a squirrel or pigeon passes through the back garden.

Position yourself under the dining room table each Sunday, before roast dinner is served.

An open dishwasher is an invitation to lick clean all the plates, bowls and cutlery.

Cats are fine if you leave them alone. Squirrels on the other hand are vicious, nasty, mischievous little critters. Plot their downfall every spare moment you get.

If you're going to eat your own sick, make sure no one's watching — they'll only try to stop you!

Always remember: cat food is just as delicious as dog food.

Dogs get a bad reputation for eating food all the time, but the truth is we require more calories per pound than humans do. When you hear the following words, it's time to get mega-excited – don't leave the dinner table unless you are being dragged away by at least four people:

🦴 Bacon/pork.

🦴 Steak.

🦴 Chicken.

If you see a baby with food all over its face, help out by licking it clean.

Hosepipes. Friend or foe? You can't be sure – keep an eye on them.

After becoming sick and tired of you humping
the legs of every piece of furniture in the house,
your human will give in and finally give you the
cherished, fluffy teddy that they were given as
a child. This will become your best friend.

Humans like to think that dog leads are put on us to control us, but really, it's for us to have fun with. To prove this, next time you are out on a walk run around your owner in circles. It's pretty funny to watch them try to untangle the lead from their legs.

You are not a pony. Remember that the next time someone wants to ride you. It's all fun and games until somebody gets hurt!

If your name is 'Bacardi' or 'Hotdog', don't worry. It's OK to be embarrassed by your name. It wasn't *your* choice.

Your family probably enjoy looking at videos of other dogs doing ridiculous things like surfing or skydiving on the Internet. To prevent jealousy attacks, spill water on the laptop and make sure you're the centre of attention.

Pigeons can fly and squirrels can climb trees. You can do neither. But don't let that stop you from chasing either in the park.

Don't ever let anyone put sponges on your feet to clean. You are not a doggy-mop. You may want to help out, but this is below you!

Over your lifetime you'll hear the following clichés spoken by your owners. Feel free to ignore them:

🦴 'We got a dog because we're not ready for kids.'

🦴 'He's actually really well trained but doesn't like performing in front of strangers.'

🦴 'The dog isn't normally allowed up on the bed.'

Humans will use you as an excuse to meet other (attractive) humans with dogs, usually during walks in the park. Help your human along by getting friendly with an attractive person's dog. This may involve a bum sniff or two, but that's OK.

When you're out in the park, the moment someone tries to take a nice picture of you is the perfect time to have a poo.

Learn to open doors with your paws. That way you'll never be far from the action.

Don't let the smell fool you – socks are not tasty.

Dog Motto #1: Good dogs go to heaven. Bad dogs go wherever they want.

Humans that don't deem themselves as 'dog people' often make insensitive remarks that may hurt your feelings. It's your duty to show them how wrong they are by humping their leg and/or slobbering over their face and clothes:

🦴 'Dogs smell too much.'

🦴 'I'm more of a cat person, to be honest.'

🦴 'Dogs are stupid.'

Your family might be tempted to create a social media profile on your behalf. You may get seven followers, but generally, it's an embarrassment for everybody. Howl with disappointment every time they post a video of you with your nose stuck in a cereal box.

Always share your food with a bigger dog.
Always steal the food of a smaller dog.
This is the doggy code.

Tip for small dogs: laptops make excellent beds – they
are very warm. If you find one that's
been left unattended, feel free to fall
asleep on it.

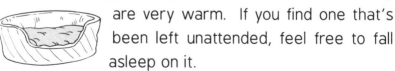

When in the presence of a human being who quite clearly is not a 'dog person', make them feel really uncomfortable for their speciesism. You can do this by:

🦴 Pooing in their shoes (usually left by the front door).

🦴 Ripping up their coat (usually left by the front door).

🦴 Not letting them in (leave them by the front door).

The concept of 'dog years' is confusing for everybody, especially dogs. Most humans think that for every one human year a dog ages seven years, but there's a simple way for them to tell the age of a dog: if you're running around full of energy, you're young. If you're slow and tired all the time, you're old.

When on the prowl for scraps at the dinner table, avoid children – their hands are too small to provide good portions.

Every dog has its day. *Yours is today.*

When playing Fetch, keep a close eye on the hand – if there is no stick, nothing will be thrown. Don't be fooled – just because somebody makes the motion of throwing a stick, doesn't mean there is a stick. Only chase real sticks, not pretend ones. Otherwise you'll look silly.

Having your poo collected in a little bag after you've done your business is a little bit embarrassing for all those involved. Find a nice wooded area and go quietly and discreetly, then move on.

Dog names can be a highly sensitive topic. However it is a little-known fact that dogs are legally allowed to change their name (via dog poll) if their names are any of the following:

🦴 Mr Dog.

🦴 Dogbert.

🦴 Spot.

A toilet roll should be dragged through the entire house and then ripped to shreds once every day.

Some human beings have cottoned on to the fact that petting a dog lowers their own blood pressure. Of course, what they tend to forget is that it increases ours. So avoid getting stroked so hard that your eyes pop out.

An instruction for all little dogs: never run alongside your owner. Run underneath them! It's funny to watch them awkwardly try to get out of your way.

Your family may bring home 'Doggy Ice Cream' one day. Ice cream for dogs! But don't eat it – it's a gimmick. You're happy just licking everybody else's bowls.

Rules for swimming in pools, ponds and lakes: ALWAYS bellyflop. Never enter gracefully.

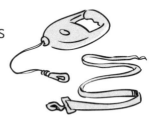

If you've been a bad dog and have been sent outside, don't worry. Put on your best 'hangdog' expression and stare through the back door. You'll be let in immediately for being too adorable!

Families get really emotionally attached to their dogs. And while you may like them a lot too, you may need to watch out for death-by-cuddles if you start to hear the following phrases:

🦴 'You're the only one who really understands me.'

🦴 'Why would I need a boyfriend when I have you?'

🦴 'What would I do without you?'

Your family will try – many, many times – to make you wear their shoes, and then get you to walk around. You'll look silly, walk silly and feel silly. Try not to indulge them.

Hairdryers are interesting and do wonders for your shaggy looks. When you hear one being used, rush immediately to it and make sure you get a good ten-minute blow-dry!

Carrying sticks ten times the size of your own body is admirable, if not practical. However, Fetch can only be played with sticks of a throwable size.

Size isn't everything: the bigger the dog, the harder they fall. Remember that next time you're in the park and a dog tries to steal your stick. Fight them to the death!

Scooting on your butt. Best enjoyed in the company of others; but even better enjoyed on an expensive carpet or rug. The newer, the better.

As part of the family, you'll
be forced to appear in the
embarrassing family portrait. Even
the humans find this embarrassing,
so do your best to look like
you are not enjoying it – you'll
fit in with everybody else.

Slobber happens. Slobber is healthy. Slobber is the sign of a happy dog. Here are three ideal places to leave thick, gooey, smelly slobber:

 **On bills and any important-looking post that's just come through the letterbox.**

On hands, faces, legs, feet – in fact, any bare human skin you see.

On chairs, so that when your family sit down, they take a piece of you with them when they stand up.

There will be some days when your owner has a Take Your Dog to Work Day. This is a treat for them. A chore for you. Misbehave as much as possible so your owner thinks twice about doing it again.

Don't look up excitedly when you hear someone say, 'it's raining cats and dogs'. It's not.

Bones are great! They may be the skeleton of a dead thing but they're fun to dig up and even better to chew on.

For every photo of you looking silly
that your family posts to Instagram,
make sure you get a treat out of it.
You're not a performing monkey.

The soap, the hot water, the sitting still – baths are just torture. Here are the three golden rules for escaping bath time:

🦴 Whenever you hear running water in the house, HIDE.

🦴 Keep on your toes. The very minute your family have picked you up, you're done for.

🦴 Be wary of the hose in the back garden. Make no mistake, it's a sneaky bath.

Give in to your suspicions. Yes, there are probably lots of doggy treats hidden inside all the cushions and pillows in the house. Rip them all open and see!

Your humans may want you to be the ring bearer at their wedding. If you act super cute and remember not to eat the ring, you'll be in doggy heaven with all the extra treats and affection.

Your owner, and in fact most humans, will be very jealous of the fact that you can lick yourself clean. Flaunt this fact – make a show of it.

Unlike chasing cats, there are a few certain rules when chasing cars:

 Cars are prone to stopping suddenly, so don't chase them too closely.

 Cars aren't squishy like cats. They hit back.

 If you did catch a car – WHAT EXACTLY DO YOU PLAN TO DO WITH IT?!

Riding along in a car with your head out the window is the best feeling in the world. If you keep your mouth open when you do it, you might get to swallow some tasty flies.

Despite being in possession of a magnificent covering of fur, your owner will still want to dress you up in a dog sweater when they have guests. Let them… it seems to make them happy.

Your owner will always spell out the word 'V.E.T.' so

as to confuse you about why you are taking a trip in the car. Any time you hear anyone say 'V.E.T.', run away.

We can hear pretty well, much better than humans. But there's no need to go mental when you hear the following:

🦴 A whistling kettle – it's just boiling water for tea.

🦴 A plane overhead – it's pretty loud for us, but it's not nearby, and it's not an intruder.

🦴 Lightning – it's scary, for sure, but it can't hurt you if you're curled up in your basket.

Never feel embarrassed for smelling a bin. Or for wanting to get inside it. You have a sense of smell at least 10,000 times better than humans — bins are heavenly.

Humping a human leg is great fun, especially if it belongs to a neighbour, or – even better – a mother-in-law.

Use your body clock to wake up everybody in the house at 6 a.m. on a Saturday morning. Don't waste the day by letting everybody sleep. Try one of these tried and tested tactics:

- Stomp heavily into your owner's room and jump up on the bed.

- Knock a pint of water onto your owner's laptop – this will wake them up!

- Bark loudly at the pesky birds in the back garden trying to invade the house.

Your owners will, at some point, want to dress you in a suit. Let them — you'll look clever!

If someone is preparing a meal you must wait for the food to come to you. Don't try to stick your face and front paws in the oven when they open it – you'll get burnt!

While it's true that we can run faster than humans, it's  also true that cats can run faster than us. While it's fun to chase them, we never catch them: give up.

Dry dog biscuits are not much of a treat. We all know this. Turn your nose up at them and wait to be offered something much fancier.

There are lots of dogs on the Internet becoming famous for their unique doggy talents. Think about what special skills you have and then practise constantly until somebody makes a video of you and posts it online.

If you need the loo in the night, remember that it takes a human many long minutes to get out of bed and put their shoes on, especially in the dark – so start scratching at the door pre-emptively to avoid having to wait until you're desperate!

A dog with healthy teeth is a healthy dog. Some doggy dentists say that a dog's teeth need cleaning every day, but that's ridiculous. You can clean and maintain your own teeth by:

 Chewing on the edges of all furniture.

🦴 Chewing on the pillows and furnishings that cover the furniture.

🦴 Chewing on anything you see that looks tasty.

Accompanying your owner on a jog. Great. Accompanying your owner on a bike ride? Forget it!

Wee at various spots in the back garden to mark your territory, and try to spray the neighbour's fence while you're there, just in case their dog gets delusions of grandeur.

Squeaky toys. Best squeaked repeatedly at 4 a.m.

Whenever your owner walks into the house, exhausted after a hard day's work, give them an hour or two to recover – this way they'll have more energy to dedicate to you!

It's very important to learn to share your things with your humans. Be generous with your muddy, chewed-up tennis ball and let them enjoy it with their next romantic, candlelit dinner. Right in the middle of the plate when their backs are turned usually does the trick.

When your owner walks through the house with umpteen bags of shopping, don't get under their feet by trying to sniff every bag and make them trip over; wait for them to put the bags down first, then stick your nose in when they're not looking.

Try these positions for sleeping, for maximum comfort and guaranteed attention from your adoring humans:

 Body on the sofa, head on the coffee table (only if table is over one foot away).

Upside down, legs stretched out – the Superman pose.

Sprawled on the kitchen floor, face in food bowl (or if you're small enough, completely within the food bowl).

If you've been out on a long, dirty walk in the rain,  traipsing through the house with muddy paws is a fun way to excite your owners.

A sure-fire way to get your owner to give you a good tug of war is to bury their TV remote – without access to their big box of moving shapes they're suddenly far more interested in playing with you.

Don't let anyone in your family take a picture of you while you shake yourself dry. We all look ridiculous when we do this.

If you're interested in finding out more about our books, find us on Facebook at **Summersdale Publishers** and follow us on Twitter at **@Summersdale**.

www.summersdale.com